Building a Marriage to Last

Five Essential Habits for Couples

Brad Hambrick

New
Growth
Press

newgrowthpress.com

New Growth Press, Greensboro, NC 27401
newgrowthpress.com
Copyright © 2020 by Brad Hambrick

Cover Design: Tom Temple, tandemcreative.net
Interior Design and Typesetting: Gretchen Logterman

ISBN: 978-1-64507-080-1 (Print)
ISBN: 978-1-64507-086-3 (eBook)

Library of Congress Cataloging-in-Publication Data

Names: Hambrick, Brad, 1977- author.
Title: Building a marriage to last : five essential habits for couples /
   Brad Hambrick.
Description: Greensboro, NC : New Growth Press, 2020. | Includes
   bibliographical references. | Summary: "Where is your marriage? You may
   find yourself be in one of several seasons-newly married, in a rut,
   coming off a major transition, or perhaps coming out of a period of
   crisis or conflict. Wherever you find yourself, you recognize that each
   season of life presents unique challenges to your relationship with your
   spouse. How can you proactively nurture your marriage in the middle of
   your particular season? Counselor and pastor Brad Hambrick encourages
   couples of all ages to intentionally adopt five core practices that can
   foster healthy, God-honoring rhythms of communication and care. Learning
   how to steward time, money, and community, practicing healthy self-care,
   avoiding criticism and defensiveness, seeking to know your spouse
   deeply, and expressing gratitude for the opportunity to grow are just
   some of the wisdom gifts from God that will help deepen your
   relationship and also call you into a deeper walk with him"-- Provided
   by publisher.
Identifiers: LCCN 2020010216 | ISBN 9781645070801 | ISBN 9781645070863
   (ebook)
Subjects: LCSH: Married people--Religious life. | Marriage--Religious
   aspects--Christianity.
Classification: LCC BV4596.M3 H36 2020 | DDC 248.8/44--dc23
LC record available at https://lccn.loc.gov/2020010216

Printed in India

30 29 28 27 26 25 24 23   4 5 6 7 8

Where is your marriage? You may find yourself in one of several seasons.

☐ Are you *newly married*, just getting started, and nervous you won't "do this marriage thing" right?

☐ Are you coming off a *major transition*—having a child, moving to a new city, or adapting to an empty nest—and not sure that what worked well for your marriage *then* will be a good fit *now*?

☐ Are you *in a rut*? Has marriage become too functional—everything is getting done but the joy you want for your marriage seems to be slowing fading into the background?

☐ Are you coming off a *season of crisis or conflict*—knowing that you want to do things *different* than before but not sure how to make sure different is also *better*?

Regardless of your situation, it's never too early—or too late, for that matter—to build habits that will strengthen and grow your marriage.

But, you might be thinking, *don't habits squelch spontaneity and make life less fun?* I mean, I get it. Life would be more *effective* with better habits, but would it be more *enjoyable*?

Those are fair questions. By personality, some people instinctively love the order and predictability of habits, while others feel squelched by routines. There may be one of each in your marriage. While this idea is more exciting to some than others, every marriage benefits from being intentional about cultivating healthy relational habits.

The reality is that you are going to forge habits in your marriage, whether you intend to or not. Habits happen as we do life. In the months ahead you are either going to *intentionally cultivate habits* that foster a healthier, more God-honoring marriage, or hope you don't *drift into habits* that result in imbalanced priorities and subsequent conflicts. Habit-forming is inevitable, but intentionality can make it beneficial.

Whatever your season of life or condition of your marriage, remember that there is no such thing as a cookie-cutter recipe for blissful marriage habits. A dozen couples could read this minibook, assess their marriages, and express these habits differently. That is a testimony to God's creative design.

One thing is guaranteed, however: if you neglect the principles here, it will be difficult for your marriage to thrive. Does that mean every healthy couple is as intentional as we invite you to be here? No. By godly examples, common sense, and trial and error, many couples develop the kind of habits we will discuss. The benefit of considering these things now is that you won't have learn them from years in the School of Hard Knocks.

When rightly understood and applied, *habits foster creativity*. This is good news for those who love to think outside the box. For example, when a couple forms the habit of a regular date night this, if done well, sparks creativity. No longer is energy spent wondering, "Will we go on a date?" Instead, the anticipation of a regular date advances the question to, "What will we do this time?" or, "What will grow our relationship?"

Habits become ruts when they become mindless. We want to avoid mindless monotony and being slaves to routine. That is why we won't talk about rote habits (i.e., brushing your teeth everyday) as much as we will meaningful practices (i.e., exercise) that allow for a variety of expressions that fit your marriage and allow for diversity in implementation. As you read, you should find lots of room for creativity and adaptation over time.

Five Essential Practices for Couples

So, are you ready to think about developing new relational habits? We're going to consider five basic categories of healthy marriage habits, covering a wide range of personal, relational, and spiritual needs:

1. Stewarding the Basics
2. Thriving Personally
3. Honoring Relationally
4. Knowing Deeply
5. Worshipping Truly

You will notice that this list begins with stewardship and ends with worship. This order is intentional.

The idea of **stewarding** comes first because it reveals that all of life, including marriage, is a gift given to us by God for a purpose. Our goal with "stewarding the basics" is to discern how God would have us care for our marriages to accomplish his purpose *in each member* of our family, *in each season* of life.

Thriving prompts us to remember that, unlike God, we are finite creatures who require certain essential elements in order to be healthy. Even before humanity was sinful (Genesis 3), we were finite (Genesis 1 and 2). People needed sleep and food even before there was a reason to repent. Here we will challenge each other to care for ourselves physically and emotionally so that our shortcomings in marriage do not stem from a lack of basic personal care.

Honoring calls us to be mindful that we are not just finite, but also sinful people who do not naturally think of others first (Romans 3:23). We want our way and are too often willing to mistreat those we love to get our way (James 4:1–6). That's not a pretty picture of the human heart, but it's an accurate one. Any discussion of a God-honoring marriage must be rooted in this kind of gospel-dependent self-awareness.

The idea of **knowing** points out that marriage requires us to be lifelong students of an ever-changing spouse. You may have heard it said, "You will be married to dozens of people over the course of your marriage." Life changes both of you. Loving your spouse entails *perpetually learning* what is more important, most challenging, and most satisfying for him or her.

Worshipping opens our eyes to see that life is not a meaningless game where the people who have the most fun and experience the least pain win. Our lives were designed to glorify God. When we lose sight of this, godly habits begin to feel like a competitive disadvantage or an arbitrary theological list of rules.

Now that we understand the purpose and order behind these essential practices, let's explore how we can build the habits of stewarding, thriving, honoring, knowing, and worshipping.

Stewarding the Basics

Marriage is not so much complicated as it is difficult. We know the destructive factors that will put a strain on our marriage, and tell other people to avoid those pitfalls. But we often dismiss important, basic marriage principles as cliché. Knowing you should work out is not the same thing as actually sweating for thirty minutes three times a week.

Let's talk about three basic commodities you need to manage in your marriage well: time, money, and community. Being overcommitted, in debt, and isolated will slowly strangle your marriage. We know this. But are we doing something about it?

Time. Let's start with this simple fact: you can't cram two hundred hours' worth of activity in to a 168-hour week and have a healthy marriage.[1] If you try, conversation will become functional (at best), quality time will evaporate, you will acquire a sleep debt, and conflict will progressively intensify.

Think monthly instead of daily or weekly. At the beginning of every month, look at your calendars together and make sure all five habit areas are present in your schedule. Make sure the things you say "yes"

7

to are the primary things that force you to say "no" to secondary priorities.

Let's be honest: not every healthy practice will be represented in every week of your schedule. But, if every healthy habit isn't represented in every month, you don't actually have habits; you have good intentions. Using a family meal calendar[2] is a great way to begin to think monthly.

Money. This idea is pretty straightforward. *Have a budget.* If, according to most surveys, the leading cause of divorce is financial problems, it would be naïve to avoid this topic. If you think of a budget as good intentions scribbled on a steno pad, learn what it means to have a working financial plan that takes less than thirty minutes a week to upkeep.[3]

Community. Your spouse should be your best friend, but not your only friend. Your spouse can't replace your church. But because God created marriage after saying, "It is not good for man to be alone" (Genesis 2:18), we often think of marriage as God's cure for loneliness. But God has made it clear that we are a part of the body of Christ and that we need to be in relationships with fellow believers for mutual encouragement and growth (Hebrews 10:24–25).

Seek out friends who model and spur you toward a healthy marriage. When you review your month each of you should ask the other, "When do you have time with [name of friend(s)] this month?" If your friendships have not been intentional toward enriching your marriage, consider inviting another couple to read this minibook with you and asking them to discuss it the next time you get together. Both the Old and New Testaments speak of the powerful influence of friendship (see Proverbs 1:8–19; 1 Corinthians 15:33).

Thriving Personally

This isn't the self-help idea, "Love yourself before you love anybody else." Thriving personally is equivalent to the preflight instruction, "Put on your air mask before you put a mask on your travel companion." Marriage is a marathon. It is a relationship that spans decades. Good self-care is a wise component of any endurance endeavor.

Your marriage will not be healthier than you are . . . at least not for long. We all know we can push the limits for a "busy season," but if we overextend as a lifestyle, we crash.

Let's exaggerate to clarify this point. If you got an average of three hours of sleep per night for the next year, how healthy would your marriage be? How attentively would you be able to listen? How much self-control would you have during conflict? How much energy would you have to pursue your husband or wife?

Establish healthy physical and emotional care habits. Look over your sleeping, eating, and exercising patterns. Are you caring for your body in a way that sets you up to care for your spouse? What one or two changes would make the biggest difference?

Now consider the unique challenges of your current season of life. Are you in graduate school, raising kids, or in a demanding job? Ask yourself, "Is there anything I need to change to have the energy and focus to engage with my spouse?" This question is a great conversation prompt for the two of you, to learn how to care well for one another in each season of life. Each of you are in a unique place to care for the other in this way. No one sees your spouse's day-in-day-out routine and how it impacts him or her like you do.

Learn your spouse's answers to these questions. When you look at your month ahead, make sure each of your thriving-personally habits are on the calendar. Periodically discussing how changes in your life affect changes in your physical and emotional care habits deepens your communication and shows care for each other.

Honoring Relationally

Now we're going to start meddling. The first two habits we looked at were about pursuing good things. This third habit is about avoiding destructive patterns. Too often, we just think about the crisis stage of destruction (i.e., adultery, bankruptcy, divorce). Here we will look at the most common precursors to crises and how to avoid them.

We will consider four put-off habits (Ephesians 4:22) for honoring one another relationally: **criticism, contempt, defensiveness,** and **stonewalling**. These four communication patterns have been identified by marriage researcher John Gottman as the most accurate predictors of divorce.[4]

- *Avoid criticism*—This doesn't mean you never express dissatisfaction or disappointment to your spouse. It means you articulate your frustration with a focus on the action or situation rather than the person. For example, instead of saying, "You never think of me. You only focus on other people and work. That's why we're always late. You just don't care about me," you might say, "It's frustrating when we're consistently late. It makes me wonder what is most important to you. Can we talk about this?"

- *Avoid contempt*—We can express contempt by mocking, name-calling, disrespectful body language (e.g., eye-rolling), or talking down to our spouses. When we communicate with contempt, we are telling our spouses that they are "less than" we are. At its best, contempt displays high levels of immaturity. At its worst, contempt reveals the early stages of an emotionally abusive relationship.[5]

- *Avoid defensiveness*—The more one spouse is critical, the more the other spouse is likely to gravitate toward defensiveness. But criticism does not excuse defensiveness. Common defensive strategies include playing the martyr and shifting the blame. Christians, more than anyone else, should be able to accept responsibility where appropriate and admit our faults. After all, acknowledging our sinful condition was a prerequisite of salvation.

- *Avoid stonewalling*—This is when we shut down and stop talking to our spouse about what is upsetting. The longer we stonewall, the more emotionally difficult stuff there is to face and the less capable we feel of facing it. It's like when we don't pay our bills: the longer we avoid paying them, the more there is to pay, and the less capable we feel to pay them. *A good marriage requires the willingness to talk maturely about hard things.*

Let's make two observations about these four destructive relational patterns.

First, these patterns are common. We know these practices are offensive and harmful. We don't like when people do them to us. But we criticize, blame-shift, and stonewall anyway. What we're talking about is sin. These are choices to dishonor our spouses when we feel uncomfortable. These aren't just "bad habits"—they're symptoms of the fallen human condition that require Jesus's life, death, and resurrection to remedy.

Realizing that interpersonal dysfunction comes from personal depravity is why this is not a "self-help minibook." Instead, it is a practical guide to why we must live Christ-reliant marriages. We will not effectively "try harder" toward better habits. We must humbly repent and ask for God to give us new hearts that respond differently to interpersonal discomfort.

Second, notice how much these four destructive patterns match the relational instruction Paul gives believers in Ephesians 4:25–32.

Therefore, having put away falsehood, let each one of you speak the truth with his neighbor, for we are members one of another. Be angry and do not sin; do not let the sun go down on your anger, and give no opportunity to the devil. Let the thief no longer steal, but rather let him labor, doing honest work with his own hands, so that he may have something to share with anyone in need. Let no corrupting talk come out of your mouths, but only such as is good for building up, as fits the occasion, that it may give grace to those who hear. And do not grieve the Holy Spirit of God, by whom you were sealed for the day of redemption. Let all bitterness and wrath and anger and clamor and slander be put away from you, along with all malice. Be kind to one another, tenderhearted, forgiving one another, as God in Christ forgave you.

Our struggles today are the same as those in the early Ephesian church, because we struggle with the same selfish bent of our hearts. John Gottman's research merely empirically confirms the points that God inspired the apostle Paul to warn the church about two thousand years ago.

A summary term for the alternative to these destructive patterns is **honor**. When we are disappointed, hurt, or offended in marriage, the mature Christlike response is to move toward our husband or wife in humility, express our concern in a way that builds him or her up, and maintain a posture that prioritizes "us" over "it" (meaning, the marriage as more important than the subject). *When we lack the ability to discuss with honor what offends us, then our lack of self-control should be a greater concern than our spouse's offense.*[6]

A way to define honor during conflict is to *accurately represent your spouse's words and actions in both tone and content.* We don't like it when people assign motives to our actions, claim to know what we were thinking, mock our statements, or misrepresent our words. These things are forms of dishonor. Honor during conflict requires dying to self (Luke 9:23–24) to avoid these tendencies when you disagree with your spouse. We begin to realize why *listening is most difficult when it is most needed.*[7]

Knowing Deeply

This is where we start to get romantic. In a healthy marriage we should be *fully known and fully loved.* The transparency of *stewarding* life together, the vulnerability of acknowledging physical weaknesses in order to *thrive*, and the humility to *honor* each during conflict coalesce into *knowing* each other deeply. You can't skip the first three habits and experience the full impact of the fourth.

We will split this habit into two sections: everyday knowing and special-occasion knowing. **Everyday knowing** includes practices you incorporate into your normal rhythms of life so that you are regularly investing in the things that are important to your spouse. **Special-occasion knowing** describes occasions where you pour more time and energy into the things that are important to your spouse (i.e., birthdays, anniversaries, Valentine's Day, marriage getaway trip, etc.).

Take some time during a date night to discuss these questions with your spouse:

- What makes you feel most loved?
- What kind of compliments (topic or style) are most encouraging to you?
- What makes a gift meaningful to you?
- If I were to arrange for you to have some alone time or time with friends, what would you prefer?
- What are the things you most enjoy doing together as a couple?
- What are the least favorite parts of your day, week, month, or year that I can help with?
- What are the best ways for me to support you in hard times?
- What are the big dreams you have for your life? How have they changed since last time we talked about them?
- What are the simple things that mean more to you now than they used to?[8]

As you and your spouse discuss these questions, realize you are not writing a to-do list. You are creating a scavenger hunt of opportunities. If you think of the conversation this way, you will enjoy the opportunities for creativity rather than be overwhelmed by expectations.

Notice that is this kind of "knowing deeply" that Paul prayed for in Philippians 1:9–11 as an expression of what abounding love looks like:

> And it is my prayer *that your love may abound more and more, with knowledge and all discernment, so that you may approve what is excellent,* and so be pure and blameless for the day of Christ, filled with the fruit of righteousness that comes through Jesus Christ, to the glory and praise of God. (emphasis added)

Worshipping Truly

Habits aren't created for habits' sake. No one works out for the sake of working out. Habits are cultivated with a goal in mind (i.e., working out to be healthy, lose weight, or make a sports team). For habits to last and remain meaningful, the reason for the habit must be worth it. That is what this final habit is about.

Let's be honest. Life is long. Marriages hit lulls. Our motivation often wanes. The payoff of investing in good marital habits doesn't always seem attractive, even if we know that its right.

Let's be even more honest. If we allow the challenges of life to cause our care for our spouses to wane, it becomes harder to garner the motivation again.

Neglecting your marriage tends to make your marriage less appealing to invest in.

Let's be brutally honest. We need something larger than the emotional payoff of "doing the right thing" to fuel our investment in healthy marriage habits. That is the core message of Ephesians 5:21–33. We are to respond to our spouse as a mirror of and expression of gratitude for how Christ loves us. The marriage covenant is a picture of the salvation covenant. Our spouse should be a primary beneficiary of our worshipful response (i.e., awe, gratitude, and obedience) to the gospel.

This is the sustaining "worth it" to motivate all that we've been discussing. Sure, it is good news and rich theology, but how does it become a habit to invest into our marriages this way? We will look at two ways worship-based motivation can become habit.

The first practice is *expressing gratitude for the opportunity to grow.* Whenever something worthwhile is hard, let your first response be a simple "thank you" prayer. Allow honesty about the challenge to be part of the "thank you." Pray something like,

> "Lord, thank you...
>
> that loving my spouse well doesn't have to be natural in order for you to love me . . .
>
> for your patience as I strive to love my spouse well . . .
>
> that I can be honest about my initial resistance . . .

that Jesus never pulled up short in his pursuit of me . . .

for being faithful even when my heart grumbles . . .

for growing me into the person who delights in growing more like you which allows me to love my spouse like you love me."

Allow gratitude to take you back to worship. Don't beat yourself up for not wanting to do what ought to be done. That's legalism. Don't aggrandize marriage or your spouse as the greatest good. That's idolatry. Instead, thank God for the character-formation work he is doing in your life through marriage. That's sanctification.

The second practice is *having enthusiasm in the moments of growth*. Hopefully, the gratitude habit (i.e., responding to hardship without grumbling) makes this enthusiasm habit (i.e., excitement for what God can do in that hard time) seem more natural. After a thank-you prayer, you should be able to more naturally shift your mindset from, "Here we go again" (i.e., dread) to "Here's our chance" (i.e., opportunity).

Too often in the difficult moments of marriage—when tensions heighten, when we're tired and work needs to be done, or when we're faced with one more monotonous chore—our first thought is, "Here we go again." This sours our disposition and sets us up to engage our spouse with dishonor.

Instead, we should think, "Here's our chance. If our marriage is going to be better [even if it's not bad], this is the kind of moment when that growth will occur." If you and your spouse couldn't do good times well, you wouldn't have gotten married. People get married because they can do good times well (i.e., laugh, tell stories, and go on dates). People *stay* married and flourish in marriage when they do hard times well (i.e., respond with honor in conflict and navigate unpleasant emotions).

Marriages that flourish respond to the difficult moments of life as opportunities to honor God and each other. When we realize this, we can become enthusiastic about opportunities to grow.

Habits of worship are the fuel that prompt you to remember that healthy marriage habits are "worth it," even when our selfishness would tempt us to believe that habits of dishonor are understandable this time. How we respond to difficult moments are the crucial junctures in healthy habit formation.

Habits versus Legalism

Legalism is the temptation to turn any good thing into a checklist. For example, God gave us the Ten Commandments in order to show our need for him (Galatians 3:19–29), but we tend to turn them into a righteousness contest. What God intended to create liberating humility we turn into a system of scorekeeping that prompts enslaving pride or debilitating insecurity.

It would be easy to do the same thing with these five marriage habits. It would be easy to become a slave to a system of habits, take pride in how well we follow the rules, fall apart when we fall short, and compete with our spouse to see who is playing the marriage game better. But that would not be life-giving.

How do we avoid a legalistic application of the principles we've discussed?

First, *enjoy these habits as wisdom gifts from God* rather than merely obeying them as rules. The advice here is more akin to Proverbs than Leviticus. It's not a legal code—it's wisdom principles. They should be applied and explored with creativity rather than obeyed with fear.

These habits are like paint: your marriage is the canvas, you and your spouse are the artists, and God is the audience. Enjoy the process of making your marriage a work of art.

Second, *remember that you always refine what you love*. To refine something is an expression of adoration, not dissatisfaction. If you love your marriage, you will seek to refine it in the ways we've discussed.

Healthy Habits and Season-of-Life Changes

But what if we begin to sense that our practice of these principles is beginning to degenerate into lifeless ruts? We're human. That will happen from time to time. How do we turn the ship?

After you have applied this material for a length of time or have entered a new season of life, it might be time to reassess how you should apply these habits. Let's briefly consider key indicators that you might need to reevaluate how you're applying these habits.

Stewarding the basics. Are you experiencing burnout? When we get overwhelmed, wise practices frequently begin to feel enslaving. This is why people don't like budgets. Budgets are wise, but we usually only consider making them when we're financially overwhelmed. Hence, people commonly think of budgets as enslaving and legalistic. In reality, budgets just express your freedom to spend your money with greater intentionally and wise forethought.

If you feel like wise marriage habits are legalistic and lifeless because you're overwhelmed, be honest about it. Be honest with yourself, your spouse, a friend, and God. *There is no shame in being a finite human being. There is a great deal of pressure in pretending you're not.* If you've gone through this minibook as a couple, your spouse has been prepared for this conversation. He or she may feel the same way and will be relieved to talk about it.

Thriving personally. Has what is life-giving to you changed? Changes in life season may alter what helps you emotionally thrive. Sometimes ruts and blah seasons are just a warning light that you've entered a new season of life. Listen to these changes. Talk about them with your spouse. Allow the quality of conversation to deepen your marriage.

Or, maybe you're doing enjoyable things in a mindless way. We've all eaten a meal while distracted and gotten no pleasure from the food. When life gets busy, we neglect being fully present in things we do to recharge. We should remember *it's not an activity that recharges us; it's the enjoyment of the activity.* The wise words of the missionary Jim Elliot apply here: "Wherever you are [whatever you're doing], be all there."[9]

Honoring relationally. Have you allowed dishonoring habits to creep back into your relationship with your spouse? When we neglect something, we don't enjoy investing in it. Neglect the upkeep of your kitchen and you won't enjoy cooking as much. When we express dishonor, investing in our marriage won't have the same emotional payoff. It will simply remind us of our need to repent.

We've talked more about active dishonor than neglect (passive dishonor). Neglect can contribute to the resentment or emotional distance we're discussing now. *A key sign of neglect is when we feel entitled to our spouses*—when we lose the sense of appreciation, gratitude, and delight in our day-to-day interactions with them. Cherishing (the opposite of entitlement) the simple moments together during the day or week can reinvigorate joy in these basic habits.

Knowing deeply. Has what is life-giving to your spouse changed? In "thriving personally" we asked this question about you. Here we are asking you to remember that the same life transitions are likely happening with your spouse.

If what is important to your spouse has changed, then you can faithfully do things that were once very enriching and get ho-hum results. Perhaps your spouse used to be recharged by an afternoon project. Now, projects may not mean as much. You adjust your calendar to give them project time, but it doesn't energize them like it used to. This is not a time to be alarmed; it's a time to talk. Marriages grow deeper when we ask, "How I've been trying to show love doesn't seem as impactful as it used to be. What's changed? What would be the best ways to love you now?"

Worshipping truly. Are you asking your marriage to fulfill you in a way that only God can? It's human nature to turn every good thing into a god. Sometimes our efforts at enhancing our marriage get distorted because we give marriage too much weight. People who get excited about reading minibooks on good marriage habits (wink, wink) may be particularly prone to this, because your marriage means a lot to you.

When marriage has taken on a weight it cannot bear, we honor our marriage best by depending on it less. This is the principle C. S. Lewis so succinctly stated, "Put first things first and we get second things thrown in: put second things first and we lose both first and second things."[10] Allow the first thing, a thriving relationship with God, to be first and then second things, such as a thriving relationship with your spouse, will have every opportunity to flourish. Ask your marriage to fulfill you like only God can and both relationships will crumble.

In each of these five areas, have fun. Be creative. God gave you marriage as a gift. God delights in seeing us cherish and enjoy the gifts he gives. Never replace the Giver with the gift at the forefront of your affections. Instead, honor the Giver by cultivating all the joy he wanted you and your spouse to have when the gift was given.

Endnotes

[1] If your marriage needs a time audit, here is a tool: http://bradhambrick.com/a-new-years-time-and-priority-audit.

[2] Brad Hambrick, "The Glorious Family Meal Calendar," April 25, 2013, http://bradhambrick.com/the-glorious-family-meal-calendar-2.

[3] Brad Hambrick, "Creating a Gospel-Centered Marriage: Finances (Podcasts)," August 28, 2017, http://bradhambrick.com/gcmfinancespc.

[4] Ellie Lisitsa, "The Four Horsemen: Criticism, Contempt, Defensiveness, and Stonewalling," The Gottman Institute, April 23, 2013, https://www.gottman.com/blog/the-four-horsemen-recognizing-criticism-contempt-defensiveness-and-stonewalling.

[5] For guidance in marriage marked by various forms of abuse, consider the resources at www.churchcares.com.

[6] For more guidance on this destructive relational pattern, consider the series "Marriage with a Chronically Self-Centered Spouse," at http://bradhambrick.com/selfcenteredspouse.

[7] Brad Hambrick, "How to Listen Well: Marital Communication 101," January 29, 2014, http://bradhambrick.com/how-to-listen-well-marital-communication-101.

[8] If you like conversation prompts like these, there are 240 conversation prompts at http://bradhambrick.com/dailytalk.

[9] "20 Powerful Jim Elliot Quotes," Leadership Resources, October 29, 2013, www.leadershipresources.org/blog/christian-missionary-jim-elliot-quotes.

[10] C. S. Lewis, "First and Second Things," C. S. Lewis Institute, July 2017, www.cslewisinstitute.org/First_and_Second_Things.